WHO WOULD WIN?®

TRICERATOPS

VS.

SPINOSAURUS

BY
JERRY PALLOTTA
ILLUSTRATED BY
ROB BOLSTER

Scholastic Inc.

*The publisher would like to thank the following for their
kind permission to use their photographs in this book:*

*Photos ©: 6: Ulrich Joger from an expedition sponsored by the Braunschweig (Germany)
National History Museum in Niger, 2006; 7: Nigel Roddis/Reuters/Corbis Images; 14:
The Natural History Museum/The Image Works; 15: Bao Dandan/Xinhua Press/Corbis Image*
*20: xijian/iStockphoto; 21 top: Mengzhang/Dreamstime; 21 bottom right: Tim Evanson/Flick.
with permission from Jack Horner, Museum of the Rockies.*

*Author note:
Triceratops and Spinosaurus lived on different continents, millions of years apart.
But what might have happened if they met?*

To my two new pals, Sloane and Shane!
−J. P.

Thank you to my beloved mother and grandmother for always encouraging me to draw!
−R. B.

Text copyright © 2016 by Jerry Pallotta.
Illustrations copyright © 2016 by Rob Bolster.

ISBN 978-0-545-68127-8

10 9 8 7 6   17 18 19 20

Printed in the U.S.A.   40
First printing 2016

Millions and millions of years ago, dinosaurs walked on Earth. What would have happened if a Triceratops met a Spinosaurus? Would they have had a fight? If they had, who do you think would win?

MEET TRICERATOPS

This dinosaur's name means "three-horned face." It was a herbivore that walked on four legs. Its mouth was shaped like a beak.

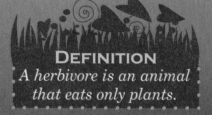

DEFINITION
A herbivore is an animal that eats only plants.

FACT
Today's alligators and crocodiles have legs that come out of the sides of their bodies.

DID YOU KNOW?
All dinosaurs had legs directly under their bodies.

Triceratops did not have an exceptionally long tail. It looked evenly balanced on all four legs.

MEET
SPINOSAURUS

Spinosaurus means "spine lizard." It had a long backbone made up of many vertebrae, or bony parts. The tall spines on its back formed a sail. Spinosaurus was a carnivore.

CARNIVORE
A carnivore is an animal that eats meat.

SIZE FACT
Spinosaurus was the largest meat-eating dinosaur. Sorry, Tyrannosaurus rex, you were smaller.

Spinosaurus lived in swamps and was probably a great swimmer. Its mouth was perfectly shaped for catching fish.

PALEONTOLOGY

Paleontology is the study of the past by digging for and learning about fossils. How do we know dinosaurs lived on Earth? While digging, people have discovered fossilized bones that are larger and different from those of animals that currently live on Earth.

This is a dinosaur fossil that was discovered by paleontologists during a dinosaur dig. Sometimes only fragments are found, and it's difficult to identify the dinosaur.

FACT
A fossil is bone, teeth, or other matter preserved by rocks and minerals for thousands or millions of years.

DEFINITION
A paleontologist is a scientist who studies the past through fossils and rock formations.

ARCHAEOLOGY

Archaeologists dig, dig, and dig to find ancient buried buildings and cities. Sometimes while excavating a site, archaeologists discover fossilized bones of extinct creatures.

Where would you rather work? On a dinosaur dig or an ancient-city dig? If you discovered a new dinosaur, what would you call it?

DEFINITION

Archaeology scientifically studies ancient peoples and cultures by excavating sites.

ELECTRONIC TOOLS

Modern tools such as satellites and sonar are used to hunt and find dinosaur fossils.

SATELLITE

A satellite beaming a signal to Earth.

SONAR

A scientist with equipment beaming sound waves at a fossil underground.

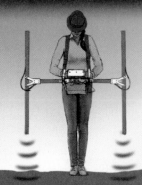

Electronic pulses and sound waves find unusual sites to start digging.

FACT
Satellites and sonar are also used to find oil and natural gas.

STANDARD TOOLS

There is no easy way to do a tough job. Eventually, paleontologists and archaeologists have to get their hands and clothes dirty. They dig with picks, trowels, and shovels.

PICKS DIGGERS BRUSHES

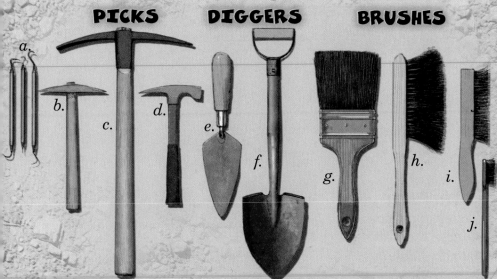

Small details are important. Big tools are eventually put aside, and brushes, magnifying glasses, and tiny tools are carefully used to preserve important information.

OPTICAL

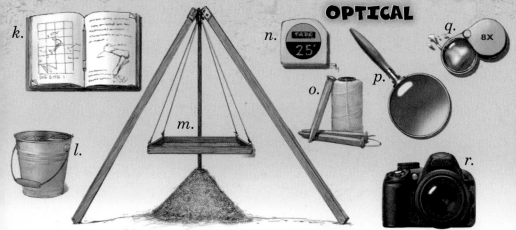

a. Dentist tools
b. Rock pick
c. Pick mattock
d. Pick hammer
e. Masonry trowel
f. Shovel

g. Paint brush
h. Dust brush
i. Wire brush
j. Toothbrush
k. Journal
l. Bucket

m. Sifting table
n. Measuring tape
o. String, stakes
p. Magnifying glass
q. Jeweler's loupe
r. Camera

BIG

How big was Triceratops? *Big!* Bigger than most elephants! Triceratops was roughly 30 feet long and 10 feet high and weighed up to 12 tons.

TRICERATOPS

TRI FACT
Triceratops was bigger than an African elephant, the heaviest land animal on Earth today.

WEIGHT CONVERSION
12 tons is equal to 24,000 pounds.

TEACHER

ELEPHANT

DID YOU KNOW?
The first dinosaur ever named was Megalosaurus.

HUGE

How huge was Spinosaurus? *Huge!* It was taller than a giraffe and longer than a humpback whale. It was about 60 feet long and weighed up to 9 tons.

SPINOSAURUS

DID YOU KNOW?
The second dinosaur to be named was the Iguanodon.

KINDERGARTNER

GIRAFFE

FUN FACT
Not all dinosaurs were huge. Some grown-up dinosaurs, such as Compsognathus, were smaller than kindergartners.

DINOSAUR

In the late 1800s, two of the most famous dinosaur hunters were busy looking for fossils. They were friends at first and then bitter rivals: Othniel Charles Marsh and Edward Drinker Cope.

> **FACT**
> *Marsh and Cope never found any dinosaur eggs.*

> **DID YOU KNOW?**
> *They never found any baby dinosaurs, either.*

They discovered well over 100 new species of dinosaurs. Books and movies have been written about these scientists.

HUNTERS

Marsh worked to find fossils for the Peabody Museum of Natural History at Yale University. Cope hunted fossils for the Academy of Natural Sciences in Philadelphia. Here are some of the species they found:

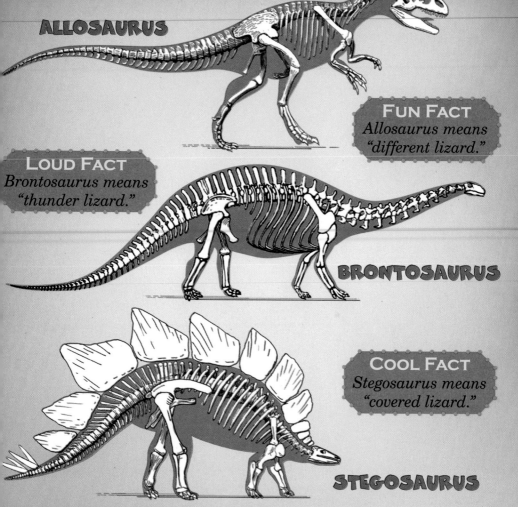

ALLOSAURUS

FUN FACT
Allosaurus means "different lizard."

LOUD FACT
Brontosaurus means "thunder lizard."

BRONTOSAURUS

COOL FACT
Stegosaurus means "covered lizard."

STEGOSAURUS

Most of the fossilized bones they discovered were in the American West, including Wyoming, Colorado, and Utah.

UTAH, WYOMING, COLORADO → W UC

UNITED STATES

TRICERATOPS SKELETON

This is a Triceratops skeleton. It was discovered in North America.

DID YOU KNOW?
Triceratops's top and bottom teeth cut like scissors, which allowed it to eat tough plants.

NORTH AMERICA

CANADA

UNITED STATES

MEXICO

Take a close look at the skeleton. Think of your own skeleton. What do you have in common with Triceratops? Its width, hands, tail, or beak? No. Four limbs, vertebrae, and ribs? Yes! Can you think of more?

FUN FACT
Dinosaurs are not the only extinct animals.

SPINOSAURUS SKELETON

This is a Spinosaurus skeleton. It was discovered in Morocco, on the continent of Africa.

MOROCCO

AFRICA

DID YOU KNOW?
Spinosaurus is thin compared to most dinosaurs its size.

Notice how skinny Spinosaurus is. Is it shaped like a fish? Take a close look. What do you have in common with this skeleton? Its sail, three fingers, or long skinny jaw? No. Its two legs and ribs? Yes! Toenails? Maybe! What else? Think!

DINO FACT
Spinosaurus was not discovered until 1912.

FUN FACT
Not all animals have skeletons!

CERATOPSIANS

Ceratopsia means "horned face." Triceratops is a member of a group of dinosaurs called ceratopsians.

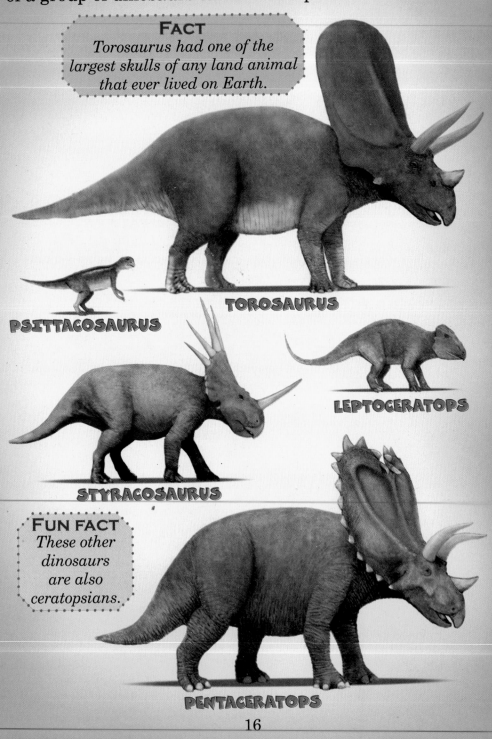

FACT
Torosaurus had one of the largest skulls of any land animal that ever lived on Earth.

PSITTACOSAURUS

TOROSAURUS

LEPTOCERATOPS

STYRACOSAURUS

FUN FACT
These other dinosaurs are also ceratopsians.

PENTACERATOPS

THEROPODS

Spinosaurs are in a group called theropods. Other theropods include Giganotosaurus, Tyrannosaurus rex, and Velociraptor.

DEFINITION
The word theropod means "beast foot."

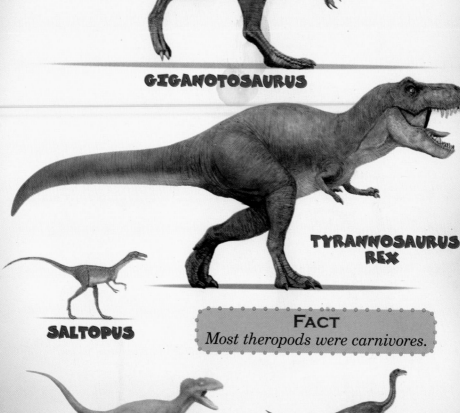

GIGANOTOSAURUS

TYRANNOSAURUS REX

SALTOPUS

FACT
Most theropods were carnivores.

VELOCIRAPTOR

GALLIMIMUS

WHAT COLOR?

Nobody today really knows what color the dinosaurs were all those millions of years ago.

FUN FACT
Color is important. It might help a dinosaur hide or find a mate. Some colors absorb or reflect light, which helps regulate a dinosaur's temperature.

DID YOU KNOW?
Most dinosaur books and movies show dinosaurs in dull or gray colors. There is no way to know if these colors are correct. Reptiles today are a rainbow of colors.

What color do you think Triceratops was? In the animal kingdom, males are often a different color than females.

WHAT DESIGN?

And there's little proof of what skin patterns the dinosaurs may have had.

MOO

Maybe Spinosaurus was patterned like a cow.

PLEASE DO THIS

Someone, please get in a time machine and come back and tell us what color the dinosaurs were.

Think of the diversity of species and colors of animals living today. The color of Spinosaurus could have been any pattern or multiple designs.

WHERE, OH WHERE?

In 1923 in Mongolia, a clutch of fossilized dinosaur eggs were discovered. But no infants or toddlers were ever found.

EGG FACT

In France in 1859, a paleontologist discovered huge fossilized eggs. He thought they were giant bird eggs. We now know they were dinosaur eggs.

It puzzled the scientific community. Where were the babies? Where were the juveniles? It was a mystery.

MEET JACK HORNER

When Jack Horner was six years old, he found his first dinosaur bone.

As an adult, Jack served as a consultant on the Jurassic Park movies.

He may be the greatest dinosaur hunter who ever lived.

WHERE ARE THE BABIES?

In 1978, Jack Horner theorized that if adult dinosaurs and predators lived along the ocean coastline, the mothers and babies must have been in the foothills.

Jack dug in the foothills of Montana. This used to be the seacoast 150 million years ago. It took a while, but he was right. The baby jawbone he examined led the way to finding a Maiasaura nursery. The fossils proved that Maiasaura took care of its young.

JUVENILE JAWBONE

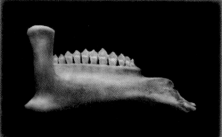

MAIASAURA EMBRYO

Jack was also the first to discover a dinosaur embryo.

SPEED

Triceratops looks slow. But it might have been a fast runner. A rhinoceros can run 30 miles per hour. Maybe Triceratops could do half that speed.

SPEED LIMIT 15

SPEED LIMIT 30

FOOTPRINTS

How do we know about dinosaur footprints? Dinosaurs walked in mud or clay, and then the mud dried and after many years became rock. Their footprints were preserved.

DID YOU KNOW?

A dinosaur footprint is a trace fossil. A trace fossil is an impression left behind by a dinosaur or other living thing.

QUICKNESS

The fastest living animal on two legs is an ostrich, which can run 45 miles per hour. Spinosaurus probably ran only about 15–20 miles per hour.

FOOTPRINTS

What did we learn when dinosaur footprints were discovered? There was no line between their feet. This meant they did not drag their tails along the ground.

FUN FACT
If you go to a national park and see dinosaur footprints, you are walking where dinosaurs once roamed.

DEFENSIVE ARMOR

Triceratops could be best described as a horned plant-eater.

SHIELD
Its head has a protective shield.

HORNS
Pointy horns.

FOUR LEGS
Being steady on four legs and well balanced is a weapon in Triceratops's arsenal.

OFFENSIVE WEAPONS

Spinosaurus has great weapons.

BITE
Long jaw with sharp pointy teeth.

SHRED
Long fingers with sharp claws.

SMACK
Long tail to smack or swim with (scientists still aren't sure).

Triceratops is busy eating green leaves. Spinosaurus is roaming around looking for food. The two dinosaurs see each other. Triceratops walks away.

Hungry Spinosaurus jogs over to attack. Triceratops runs away. This plant-eater does not want to fight.

Spinosaurus easily catches up and bites Triceratops.

Triceratops turns and faces Spinosaurus. The two dinosaurs push each other back and forth.

Triceratops charges Spinosaurus. They fight ferociously.

It is agility versus bony head frills; teeth and claws versus horns.

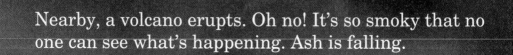

Nearby, a volcano erupts. Oh no! It's so smoky that no one can see what's happening. Ash is falling.

Ash and lava bury the two dinosaurs. But what happened?

It's one hundred million years later. We are on a dinosaur dig. The paleontologists have unearthed dinosaur fossils. Who won the fight? Turn the page for the answer.

WHO HAS THE ADVANTAGE? CHECKLIST

TRICERATOPS		SPINOSAURUS
☑	Size	☐
☑	Speed	☐
☑	Horns	☐
☐	Claws	☑
☑	Weight	☐
☑	Armor	☐

Author's note: This is one way the fight might have ended. How would you write the ending?